"When abroad – do as the local children do"

Ori's guide for young expats

Hilly van Swol-Ulbrich

Bettina Kaltenhäuser

Imprint

Editor:	CONSULT*us* Expatriate Briefings & Intercultural Seminars GmbH 65719 Hofheim www.consultus.net
Authors:	Hilly van Swol-Ulbrich Bettina Kaltenhäuser
Translated and adapted by:	Hilly van Swol-Ulbrich
Illustrations: Layout and design:	Michael Malm Sanja Galic
Printing:	Snoeck-Ducaju & Zoon, Ghent, Belgium
Publisher:	XPat Media, the Netherlands www.xpat.nl

ISBN 90 5594 262 6

We dedicate this book
    to all migrating birds,
large and small.

About the authors:

Hilly van Swol-Ulbrich

has an English mother, a Dutch father and a German husband. Before she moved to Germany, she lived in the Netherlands and in the United Kingdom. After a dozen moves, she founded a relocation agency in the Netherlands in 1987. Five years later she established CONSULTus Expatriate Briefings & Intercultural Seminars, a training company in Hofheim, Germany.

As a specialist for customised intercultural training, Hilly has gathered more than 10 years of experience. In her opinion the international move impacts children in its own distinct way. The concerns of the mini expats and the wish of the parents to make their children benefit from the international and multicultural environment have been the stimulus to publish this book.

The ever-growing flock of migrating birds has been a constant source of inspiration. Have a good flight!

Bettina Kaltenhäuser M.A.

studied publishing and psychology, which enabled her to get to know the faculties of universities in Italy, Switzerland, the USA and Germany.

In all these countries she encountered differences that went beyond just typical foods i.e.: pasta, cheese raclette, hamburgers and sauerkraut.

Upon her return to Germany she incorporated these intercultural experiences into her private and professional life.

Bettina prepared herself mentally for the unexpected each time she went abroad; it is this important trait and characteristic she wants to communicate to the children. Feel encouraged to bite off your own personal piece of the adventure abroad. Bon appétit!

Your "Navigator" for using this book:

Dear parents / instructors,
page 92 and onwards provides
* information regarding the concept of this book
* concrete advice on how to ease the move and the transition period abroad relating to chapters 1-8
* recommendations in a Ten-Point Action Plan
* list of further resources

Hello and welcome to your book

old home

new home

You are entering an interesting and exciting time, you will get a second home abroad! In this book you will find many ideas on how to make this move abroad a rewarding experience and an unforgettable adventure.

How can we possibly know this? Ori, the migrating bird, is our international moving specialist. He has gathered his ideas and stories in this workbook filled with assignments. Regardless of when you use this book – before the move, on the road, or in the new home abroad – you will find lots of opportunities to enjoy yourself whilst you try out the many tips and activities!

Ori would like to get to know you on the next pages. When you have found Ori's address, drop him a line …
Let him know what you think of his ideas, share your ideas or simply tell him how you are!

Enjoy!

"Pleased to meet you"

1. Your life until now ...

was just normal. Maybe you have not given it a lot of thought, right? Everyday things are taken for granted, but you will leave your everyday life behind you. So let's get started with something simple and yet very important: you, your family and your friends.

Remember, now there is Ori, the rather inquisitive migrating bird, who is really eager to learn about you.

"Hi, it's me, Ori!

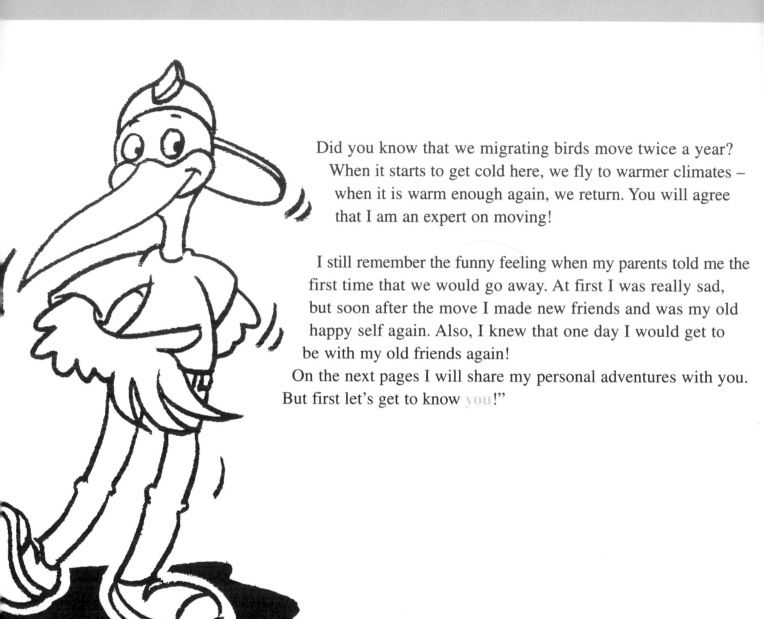

Did you know that we migrating birds move twice a year?
When it starts to get cold here, we fly to warmer climates –
when it is warm enough again, we return. You will agree
that I am an expert on moving!

I still remember the funny feeling when my parents told me the
first time that we would go away. At first I was really sad,
but soon after the move I made new friends and was my old
happy self again. Also, I knew that one day I would get to
be with my old friends again!
On the next pages I will share my personal adventures with you.
But first let's get to know you!"

This is about me!

My picture

My name

_____

My address

_____

_____

My age

_____

I am moving to

_____

My special interests are

_____

_____

Any sport or hobbies?

When you spot yours mark the picture. If not, why not draw your favourite hobby / sport in the box?

This is an apple tree, but it is also a family tree

For each family member draw an apple and write their name by it.

Old home

Your house is very special to you. Draw your favourite place in or around the house, or paste in a picture and mark the location. Is it your room or do you have a secret hiding place?

Here you can paste a picture of your family and write down what makes them special. Should you remember a funny situation, then use this to write a small story.

No problem,
    I'll get it sorted!

2. Your preparations for the move

The list of things to do is a mile long when you move. Because of all the organising we may even forget why we are going in the first place! Of course we do not want you to forget your favourite items, but let's take a moment and answer the next questions.

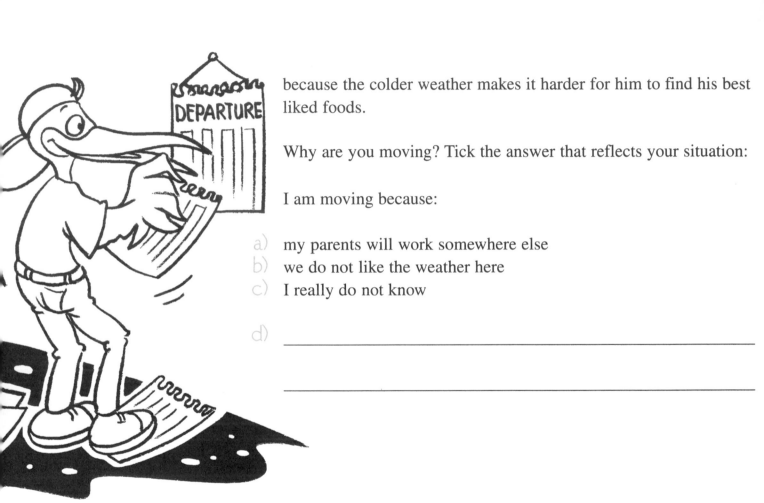

because the colder weather makes it harder for him to find his best liked foods.

Why are you moving? Tick the answer that reflects your situation:

I am moving because:

a) my parents will work somewhere else
b) we do not like the weather here
c) I really do not know

d) _____

_____

Should you have picked c) then best go and ask your parents!

Many children have packed their suitcases and boxes

a) Do you know any children who have moved abroad?

Name: _____

b) In many books you can read about children's adventures in foreign lands.

Maybe you have read these books?

* The Wizard of Oz   * Alice in Wonderland
* Nils Holgersson   * Peter Pan

c) What was interesting or funny about these stories?
What do you admire about these children?

_____

_____

Visit www.iecc.org the intercultural E-mail Classroom Connection is represented in 85 countries – your chance to find out about your new destination and the kids who live there!

Draw a face to show how you feel, don't forget your hair!

Which expression does the face show?

○ happy
○ sad
○ angry
○ neutral,
  don't care either way

Why do you feel that way?

_____

What would Dorothy, Nils, Peter or Alice say to you if you had a chance to talk to them?

_____

What is on your mind? Mark your box!

1. Are you worried about being without your present friends in your new country?

   ○ Yes, I am really scared to be without friends.
   ○ I'll wait and see.
   ○ No, I am sure I will find new friends.
   ○
   _____

2. What about your hobbies and personal interests?

   ○ I will have to give them up, what a shame!
   ○ Maybe I could find a way to continue some of them...
   ○ I would not mind trying out something new.
   ○ I am sure there are interesting alternatives!
   ○
   _____

What is on your mind? Mark your box!

3. Things I look forward to and things I will not miss at all:

○ I don't look forward to anything at all!
○ I am not sad to say goodbye to my teacher, or the barking dog in the neighbourhood, or

_____

(fill in the blank)

○ I look forward to my new country, because I can

_____

(fill in the blank)

○

_____

 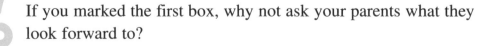 If you marked the first box, why not ask your parents what they look forward to?

were a little sad at first when I told them I would be leaving. But after we spoke about my new country, they were really excited and even wanted to come along!"

How did your friends react?

○ I'll come and visit you!

○ I have moved in the past as well!

○ What is it like?

○ I'll miss you!

○ I have been there!

○ Great!

○ _____

Those boring moving preparations!

Reality check! Some are not so bad ...
Mark the boxes as you finish off the list!

☐ Return books and / or borrowed items

☐ Sort out

☐ Cancel memberships

☐ Stay overnight at _____

☐ Write an article for the school paper

☐ Deliver on the promise you made to _____

☐ Organise a goodbye party

☐ _____

☐ _____

With a time capsule you can leave important information for future archeologists! When you return, it is fun to see the changes!
Take a solid box. Choose some personal items. Put them in the box and mark it with your name and date. Bury it in a secret place!! Make sure you make a treasure map, so you will find it again. When you return home, dig it up and enjoy seeing some familiar things and also notice what has changed.

Moving made easy!

What do these two animals have in common?

_____

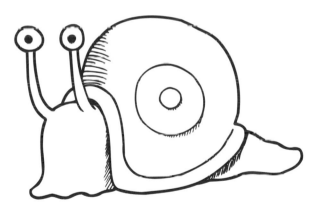

What is it that you need to do that these two friends above don't?

_____

What items will I put in my personal boxes

starting with the letter A ...

A •••	J	S
B ••	K	Times
C •	L	U
D	M	U
E	N	W
F	O	X
G ood	P	Y
H	Q	Z
I	R	

Did you prepare your stickers for the boxes?
Here is a suggestion:

You can copy this onto stickers or create your own! Also ask the removal company, they may have some very good designs!

This box belongs to: _____

Contents: _____

Where to put: _____

○ Very important Remarks: _____

○ no hurry _____

28

Your personal space for
your pictures and notes

Forever friends

3. Old and new friends

Of course you would like to say goodbye to your present friends. Not to worry; there are so many ways to stay in touch! And in your new country it is not too hard to make new friends.
Ori has put together some of his many ideas, and has even hidden his own address. Let's see whether you can find it...

Ori's friends left a personal message in his scrapbook – you can tell how much this pleases Ori!

Below are some creative ideas of things your friends and other important people like grandparents can put in your book:

Here is your personal friendship scrapbook >>

fingerprints, leaves from a tree, pictures, photos, dried flowers, proverbs or sayings, song texts, funny jokes.

Name:

Name:

Name:

Name:

Name:

Name:

Ways to stay in touch and up-to-date!

You can:

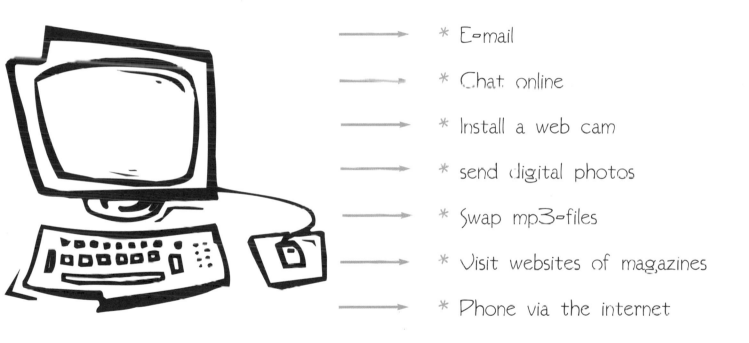

→ * E-mail

→ * Chat online

→ * Install a web cam

→ * send digital photos

→ * Swap mp3-files

→ * Visit websites of magazines

→ * Phone via the internet

! * Create a family homepage, so all your friends can check in and see how you are.
   How? Easy instructions provided by Hotdog junior: www.sausagetools.com/junior
  * Looking for great clip art for your site? Go to www.kidsdomain.com/clip
  * Also visit www.yahooligans.com this is a cool search site for young internet users.
  * Discuss with your grandparents which way they prefer to communicate with you.

VIP. e-mails

✂

Name: Ori

Address: 2, The Nest

E-mail: Ori@Ori-and-Ricki.net

Name:

Address:

E-mail:

Name:

Address:

E-mail:

Name:

Address:

E-mail:

Name:

Address:

E-mail:

Name:

Address:

E-mail:

Name:

Address:

E-mail:

Name:

Address:

E-mail:

Not enough? Then copy the page before you ask friends to write in your book.

Your personal
calling cards

✂

Name:	Name:
Address:	Address:
E-mail:	E-mail:
Name:	Name:
Address:	Address:
E-mail:	E-mail:
Name:	Name:
Address:	Address:
E-mail:	E-mail:
Name:	Name:
Address:	Address:
E-mail:	E-mail:

You may want to copy this page and then cut out the individual cards. Hand them over to your friends stating **your** new address details.

Ori is folding paper figures. Cranes, of course! These majestic migrating birds are a symbol of hope and good luck in Japan. The art of folding paper figures is called origami.

Ori thinks it makes a great farewell gift for special friends. Would you like to try your hand at it? You will be remembered by your friends each time they see the crane. Why not fold the cranes on your last school day and have the whole class join in the fun? Lots of origami!

How to fold a "good luck" crane

Ori did it! … Now it is your turn – the art of origami has many more figures for you in store! Check out the reference in the resource section in the back of this book.

Just follow the instructions and have a little patience.

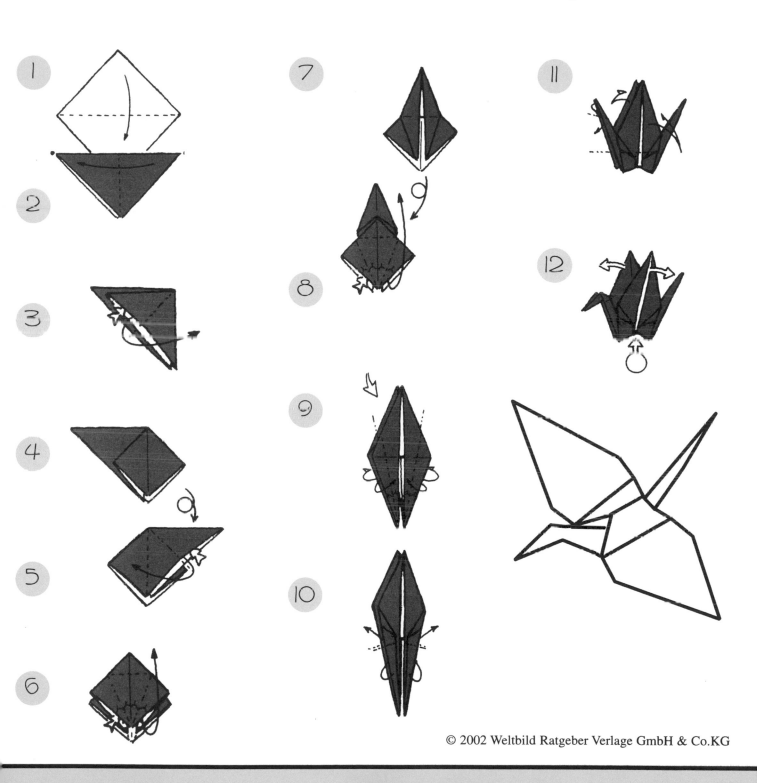

Finding new friends isn't too hard!

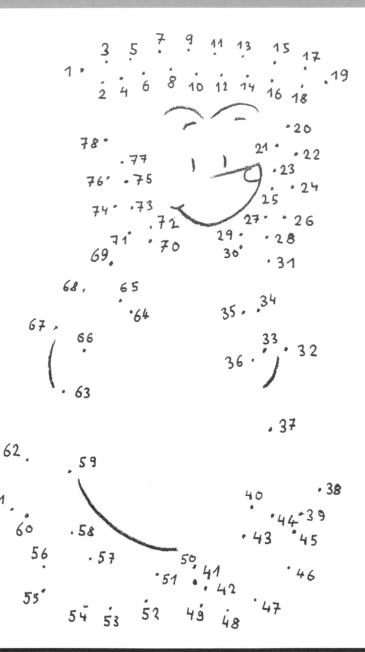

The real exciting thing about moving is the opportunity to see new things and make new friends.

In the beginning some of the new kids may be holding off, and even you might be a bit shy. Give it time and you will see that once you get to know each other a little better these kids are actually very friendly.

Ori knows all about it! At first, he thought his new friend was rather prickly.

But now they are the best of friends.

Connect the numbers and you will find Ricki is a

_____

Where to find new friends?
... un-scramble this alphabet salad!

SPRTSCBLUO: _____

CSHLOODANB: _____

CHRCHU: _____

STUOCS: _____

THTREAEGPROU: _____

PPRAESCLOOH: _____

RIOHC: _____

SATEERLUNVOA: _____

Solutions:
sportsclub, school band, church,
scouts, theatre group, school
paper, choir, as a volunteer

Did you ever ...
* Once in your new country: attach a postcard with your
  mailing address to a balloon and just let it fly off into
  the sky! Who will find it and who will answer?
* Or visit the website www.scout.net

43

Lots of fun without a lot of words!

1. Create clever figures with finger **string games** and learn some new ones from a new friend. You don't need a lot of words.

2. Ever played the game called **memory**? Take a camera and take photos of everyday life. This can be a mailbox, a school, a supermarket, your house – pictures from everything around you. Make sure you have identical pairs, that is to say, two of each. Shuffle the pictures and place them face down. Take turns in finding the matching pairs. The person who finds a matching pair continues, till they don't make a match. This is a fun way to show where you come from.

3. The **mirror game** is so easy and yet such fun. Kids face each other and copy each others' movements, but with the utmost precision and concentration. The first one who laughs, loses!

Did you know that finger string games are played all over the world? A variety of other great international games is listed in the back of this book.

Your personal space for your pictures and notes

Explorers — on your marks;
ready, steady, go!

4. Your new country

Curious about your new country?

Ori will share some of his special sources – here you will find loads of information.
Having done your research you can then prepare a list of important questions for your parents. You will see that the more you know before you go, the easier the move will be.

So, what are we waiting for ...?

My new country

is called ...

Draw the outline of your new country and fill in details such as mountains, sea, rivers, cities. Fill in what you know and don't hesitate to use an atlas!

* http://sunsite.berkeley.edu/kidsclick offers excellent details on most countries worldwide.
* www.thinkquest.org has fun activities and e-pals by country.
* www.national geographic.com/kids can help you with this research activity.

Where is your new country in relation to where you live now?

Use the compass to indicate it's position.

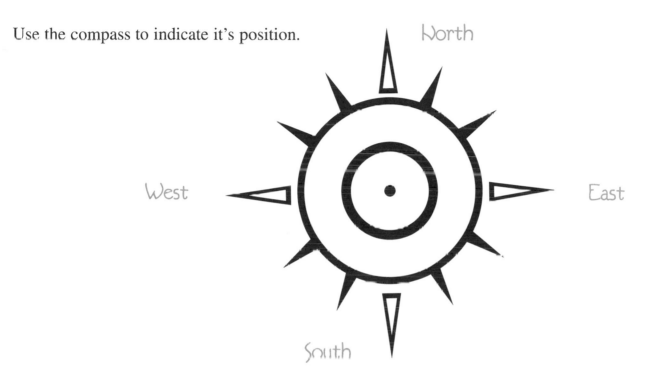

Note down the longitude and latitude as well.

_____

For the astronomers among us: are there any particular stars or constellations that can be observed clearly?

_____

It's about time!

Oops, is there a time difference between the two countries? Let's see, when the clock says 10.00 A.M. at your present home, what is the time in your new country? Will both countries have the same date on the calendar?

Date: _____

Date: _____ Time: _____

At home

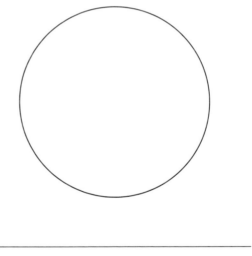

_____
In my new country

 For help visit website: www.hilink.com.au/times

World passport

Your new country's flag

Paste in a picture
of the flag

A stamp from your new country.

Paste in a
postage stamp

Paste in Ori thumbs up
icon, see page 53

Well done!

Do you also know....

A special animal in your new country?

> Paste in an animal
> picture

A popular sports figure in your new country?

> Paste in a picture
> of a sports figure

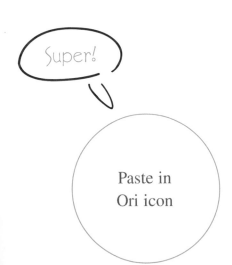

Super!

Paste in
Ori icon

A typical girl's name?

_____

A typical boy's name?

_____

Ori says: "Great job!"

Cut out the 3 smaller Ori icons and paste them in on pages 51, 52 and 54!

This larger Ori icon is for later. Cut out once you have completed page 85.

Money talks

What is the name for your new pocket money?

_____

Name the currency and its denominations:

_____

(example: Euros and Cents)

How much would your present allowance be in the new currency?

> Room for calculations

Well done!
Congratulations with your
new passport.

Ori icon

Say what?

Do you and your friends have your own secret language that you share with no one else? Then you will no doubt enjoy learning your new language. Maybe you want to try your hand at some words?

Please

_____

Thank you

_____

Good morning,

_____

Good night

_____

Hello

_____

Goodbye

_____

One

_____

Five

_____

Tips to master a new language:
* write the new words for everything in your room on Post-it notes and stick them on the relevant objects: the word for bed on your bed, the word for chair on your chair, for lamp, for desk, for closet etc.
* Greet your parents in the new language every day.

55

"Food for thought"

Take your pick,
mark the right answer!

1. What do people eat for breakfast?

   ○ Fried eggs   ○ Mashed beans
   ○ Raw fish   ○ _____

2. At what time is dinner?

   ○ 13.00   ○ 8.00 p.m.
   ○ 22.00   ○ _____

3. Any special meals to eat on public holidays?

   ○ Special cake & pastries   ○ A special soup
   ○ Specific sort of meat   ○ _____

4. What tools (cutlery) are used at the table?

   ○ Knife and fork   ○ Hands only
   ○ Chopsticks   ○ _____

5. Any particular food that is considered taboo?

   ○ Pork   ○ Cheese
   ○ Beef   ○ _____

Try one new recipe per week, maybe you can assist with the preparations! Book tip: "a Passport on your plate" Test your gourmet knowledge with an international quiz at www.berlitz.com/kidtalk

Party, Feier, Fiesta

What special holidays await you in your new country? Does one celebrate a birthday or a name day? What about Christmas, New Year's Eve, and …

Who is invited?

_____

Are gifts given?

_____

What meal is served?

_____

Which songs are sung?

_____

What do people wear?

_____

The most special event is:

_____

* For a world wide overview of holidays and celebrations visit www.earthcalendar.net
* Throw a party after the move and ask everyone invited to wear their national costume. Including yourself!
* When you attend a celebration in the new country take a tape recorder. But do ask for permission when you record others.

Your personal space for your pictures and notes

After your move write an eyewitness report on a special festivity
and send a copy to kids@holidayfestival.com

Your personal space for your pictures and notes

Paste in an entrance ticket, for instance: the zoo, the theatre, the cinema, etc.!

"Good preparation
            is half the work"

5. What will change?

Most of the time surprises are good fun. However, when moving abroad, it helps to spot changes ahead of time, so that we are prepared to enjoy them and the many other unexpected experiences ahead of us.

Changes at a glance.

Write down in the first column what remains the same, in the second what will change, and in the third what you can do about it.

	remains	will differ	I'll change
Example Your room:	wall posters	size	decoration
House / apartment Your room Garden / balcony Amount of space Neighbours			
Direct area Sports facilities Fields / woods / parks Shopping facilities Public transport			
School Getting to school School uniform School subjects School lunch / cafeteria			

 Have you been given special home work projects from your "home school" or do you just want to make sure you stay on track with the curriculum? A little help is available under **www.startribune.com/education/homework** Should you want to communicate with other homeschooling kids check out: **www.rsts.net/home/epals**

My weekly schedule

Consider what would be a typical routine in your new country.
Do not hesitate to ask your parents for help.

Mon	Tue	Wed	Thu	Fri	Sat	Sun

 Send your new class an e-mail to introduce yourself. You could even include a scanned picture. Why not write about your present schedule, this will allow your new classmates to get to know you before you are even there. Their reply will be interesting, don't you think?

What remains the same — regardless of where you are?

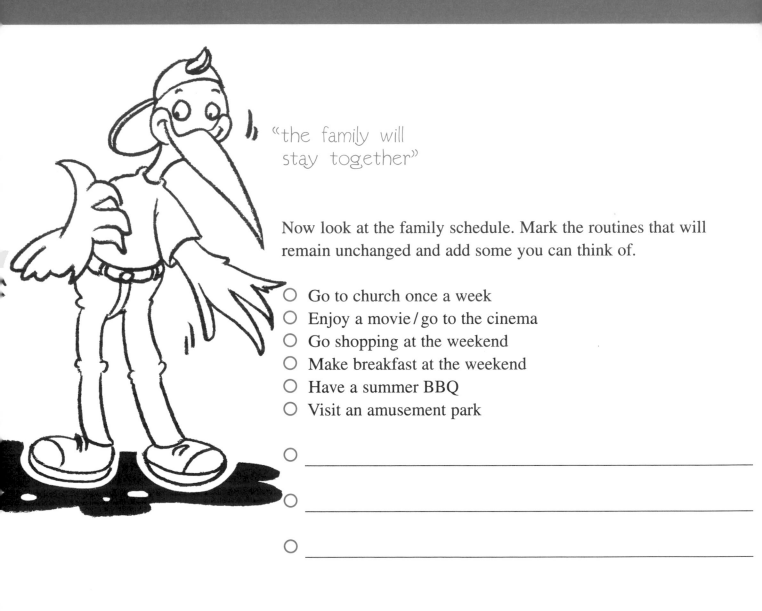

"the family will
stay together"

Now look at the family schedule. Mark the routines that will remain unchanged and add some you can think of.

○ Go to church once a week
○ Enjoy a movie / go to the cinema
○ Go shopping at the weekend
○ Make breakfast at the weekend
○ Have a summer BBQ
○ Visit an amusement park

○ _____

○ _____

○ _____

In any new country there are things that appear different, even strange at times. The same applied for Ricki und Ori, before they became friends. The first thing they noticed about each other were the differences. Then Ori just pulled himself together and asked Ricki: "What is this special fur on your back?" And Ricki answered: "That is not fur – these are my spines, they protect me in case of danger." Now it was Ricki's turn and he asked "Why do you have such a long nose?!" Here Ori put him right: "That is not a nose – that is my beak. I use it to search for food." Now that both of them understood why they looked different, they could laugh it off and even imagined what Ori would look like if he had spines on his back and what if Ricki had Ori's beak. But both came to the conclusion that they were fine just as they were and decided to become friends. People are less patient when they do not understand certain things, especially when confronted with the unknown. Maybe you could think back about Ori and Ricki the next time you are in a new situation. When you meet another child or any person and notice that they either behave differently or look different, don't be impatient. Learn from observation as well as from asking politely. There are usually very good reasons why things or people look and/or behave differently from what you consider to be "normal". You might even want to try out some things that, however different, will no longer be strange once you understand them.

1, 2, 3, 4, 5 senses!

Hands/feel
touch a new fabric or note the temperature.

Ears/ _____
listen to children's songs or fairytales from the new country.

Eyes/ _____
have a contest: who spies the first mailbox? Take a picture.

 Listen to various national anthems: www.countryreports.org

Nose / _____
dry and press one of the local flowers and paste it in.

Tongue / _____   _____
describe your new best liked breakfast food.

* Take the recipe of your present favourite meal. Check the availability of the needed ingredients. Maybe you can cook it at the new school or with your new friends at home.

* Just a word of caution. Before you pick flowers make sure that they are not on the list of protected species or have a ritual meaning. Best to ask an adult which flowers are okay for you to pick.

Of course it helps when you clean up your room, but what else can you do?

How about being a little more on your mark; more than usual?!
When abroad even unsuspected things will need your careful attention ...

CAREFUL! – when crossing the road!
Does traffic drive on the same side of the road?

CAREFUL! – when swimming!
Never jump / dive into unfamiliar waters.

ATTENTION! – when picking unknown plants / flowers!
Do some of them cause allergic reactions?

ATTENTION! – when you see unknown animals!
Do not pick up or feed without parent's consent.

Your personal space for
your pictures and notes

Safety COMES first

* **Local emergency telephone numbers:**

  _____

* **Work telephone number of parents:**

  _____

  _____

* **Parents' private address and telephone number:**

  _____

  _____

* **Telephone number of a trusted friend:**

  _____

  _____

* **Special health concerns:**

  _____

* **Known allergies:**

  _____

* **The medication I take is:**

  _____

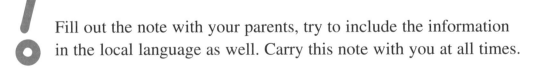

Fill out the note with your parents, try to include the information in the local language as well. Carry this note with you at all times.

Your personal space for your pictures and notes

Sure, I will be fine,
     but right now ...

6. ... I just feel like leaving!

Moving is not only fun. Sometimes you just don't know where you really belong any more. Ori knows that feeling too. He spoke to his friend Ricki about it. Ricki has a few suggestions for you.

Do YOU know that feeling?

Ori got a letter … He wants to be alone

Ori has the blues;
"Will they forget me?"
"Wish I was there"
"I am bored"
"I am sad"
"Everything is so different"

Ricki's
advice corner

Ori says: "I don't feel at home, everything is different!"

Ricki's advice: "Don't be shy of asking questions. A good way to get answers is by using the reporter's questionnaire on **page 77** – now it is more like an interview! This way of asking questions is much more fun!"

Ori says: "I don't know what to do, I am bored!"

Ricki's advice: "Clean out the last of your moving boxes, you may be surprised by what you find."

Ori says: "I dread the first day at the new school."

Ricki's advice: "Take the Global Three-in-a-Row sheet with you (see **page 78**). This activity is a fun way to get to know the other kids."

If you should feel like Ori, why not keep a diary or a **secret** journal. You can write about all the things that have happened and what your feelings were. Your personal sheets for copying are on the next page.

My secret diary

Date: _____   This journal belongs to: _____

_____

_____

_____

_____

_____

_____

_____

_____

_____

_____

Need more pages?
Copy this one before writing

Imagine yourself being an eyewitness **reporter**, like a foreign correspondent abroad working for a newspaper. This is your ticket to ask the questions that really interest you.

Come up with 8 questions and take a tape recorder with you. Your questions can relate to sports, preferred places to eat with children, etc.
Here are some examples:

1. What is your favourite TV programme?
2. Where do you go to swim in the summer?
3. How do you like to spend your leisure time?

_____

_____

_____

_____

_____

_____

_____

Write a report and put it on your family website. Submit your article to the web administrator of: www.kidsreport.com an online newspaper by kids for kids.

Global Three-in-a-Row

Find someone who fits the description in one of the boxes. A different person must sign each box. The object is to have three different names in a row vertically, horizontally, or diagonally. Once you have done this call out "Three in a row!" Easy? Then finish the page!

Who plays soccer?	Who has travelled to another country at least twice?	Who has grandparents living in the United States?
Who can speak and understand Spanish or German?	Put your name in this box.	Who comes from a family of four or more children?
Who has been skiing in Switzerland?	Who has had his or her name in the newspaper?	Who has slept overnight on a train?

Of course you can adapt the questions, and should you need help with translation into your new language, ask your teacher for advice.

"How could I forget the many things I looked forward to?!"

And you?
Flip back to **page 24**. For more ideas, try one of these ...

* A **video project**: Be a film director and video tape (or film) "A typical day in the life of ..."

* Go on a **photo safari** and take pictures of all the special things you have noticed.

* Schedule the **visit** for your friend from your first home country; what will you do and where will you go?

* Send a **message in a bottle** with your personal notes and throw it into a stream or river, but make sure it is watertight.

* Organise a **treasure hunt** for the next weekend!

Ori wants to enjoy the view from your window!

On certain days you may prefer to be alone, just by yourself. That will be the perfect time to create your own Ori figure and attach it to your window. You need this print, a pair of scissors and the usual window color® painting necessities ... Have fun!!

Your personal space for
your pictures and notes

Ready for take off?

7. Looking back

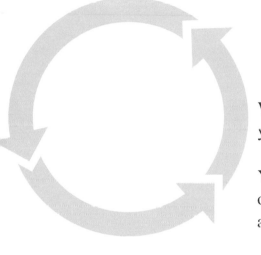

Well done! You have learned a lot about moving but also about your new country.

You worked out an action list and have tried your hand at some of the activities that helped you to get to know your new country and your place in it.

This is the time to take a moment and be proud of what you have accomplished so far. It is Ori's pleasure to document this with your personal achievement certificate. It will motivate you to continue learning and exploring the unknown.

Fill in your migrating bird certificate. Frame it and hang it above your desk.

Each time you look up, you will remember your achievements as well as your intentions.

Gute Reise!
Safe Journey!
Bon Voyage!
Goede Reis!

Have your picture taken holding the certificate and send it to your grandparents. They will enjoy sharing this important moment with you, don't you think?

Migrating bird certificate

I intend to _____

_____

I never thought that _____

_____

I will continue to _____

_____

I have learned to _____

_____

If I had one wish, I _____

_____

_____

Ori's Icon
see page 53

Place_____ Date _____

Signature _____

When you have
a good time...

8. Time flies!

As an official member of the migrating bird community, you know the moment will come to return to your first home country. For some of the other migrating birds, their journey takes them even further, to yet another destination, before they too return.

Whether you are on your way back or whether you are off to a new adventure, the next pages will guide you to making the most of this special period in your life.

How to return
and feel at home

Your friends will be happy to welcome you home again. To make sure that you fit right in, consider that it is important to stay in touch and to be up-to-date with the following:

* Music, videos and music charts.
* Fashion or the cool ways to dress.
* The expressions that are in or out.
* The hot TV shows or sitcoms.
* The latest computer / Gameboy games.
* The latest developments at your old school.

Check out the changes and share some gossip in the chatroom of www.K12nation.net or www.cybersleuth-kids.com

a) Write what you liked best about your second home country:

_____

_____

_____

b) What skills or achievements have you mastered?
A new language, new sport, a special game?

_____

_____

Paste in a picture of your best
friend from your second
home country

 Make a treasure chest to take home and fill it with your best memories of your second home country: pictures of the house, the school, your friends, postcards from the places you visited. Do not forget wrappers of your favourite snacks, maybe a newspaper, anything that is important for you. Of course you can go back to chapters 3, 4, 5 and complete the cycle.

Your personal space for your pictures and notes

Gute Reise!
Safe Journey!
Bon Voyage!
Goede Reis!

Although Ori and Ricki are saying goodbye, they will remain friends and exchange their personal stories. This way they will stay in touch. Ori looks forward to also hearing from you and about your adventures.

Ricki welcomes your contributions to his "Advice Corner", so that others can benefit from your experiences.

Take care and – Bye Bye!

9. Information for your parents / instructors

Here we present:

* the interactive concept of this book.

* suggestions per chapter to alleviate the stress of the move and to master the challenges of the adaptation phases.

* important observations in a Ten-Point Action Plan.

* further resources: books, websites, games and activities round out this book.

The why,
what and how

Target readers:

This book is directed at families with children aged 8-12 who are moving abroad.

Aims and objectives:

The book channels the creativity of the children and supports playful yet concrete preparation for the changes connected with living abroad. It invites children not only to question situations and identities, but also to reflect upon how the child is affected by being uprooted. It encourages initiative in exploring the opportunities as well as the challenges of the new environment. The interactive format presents many activities which identify things that the child can control and passes on a sense of mastery that is beneficial during the more challenging phases of an international mobile childhood.

A generic approach:

An expatriate assignment – regardless of which destination is involved – affects both children and adults. This book therefore concentrates on the process rather than on a specific country. The focus is on conscious preparation and a generic cultural awareness and sensitivity.

Country specific information:

The website **www.Ori-and-Ricki.net** offers a selection of links for both adults and children. Country specific information is presented in the form of links; this is supplemented by a country specific bibliography of recommended books. These resources allow readers to build a basic understanding of the cultural challenges connected to their foreign destination.

The emotional side of the move: The aspirations and concerns of children differ from those of the parents. Reading and working through the book together will let the parents gain direct access to the feelings of the children. Knowing their needs, support can be offered to develop and/or implement coping skills during the transition phases. The migrating bird Ori leads the child through this book and is an identification figure throughout the process. Ori conveys the sense of active involvement and can be reached by e-mail **Ori@Ori-and-Ricki.net** for feedback, but also for questions.

Structure and use: The organisation of this book is structured upon the distinct phases to be experienced when moving abroad. (Hormuth 1988: 2-3):

1. Realisation of the present, life at home   (Chapter 1)
2. The preparation phase before the move   (Chapters 2-3)
3. The critical phase after the move   (Chapters 4-7)
4. Moving on – repatriation   (Chapter 8)

This book carries recommendations and suggestions for the different phases. We encourage the involvement of parents, relatives, guardians, teachers and intercultural trainers in order to gain the utmost from this tool and to ensure that its contents are used during the different phases of the transition. Also, the authors aspire to contribute a positive spirit of anticipation for the whole family. Please let us have the benefit of your opinions; **we look forward to your feedback!**

Comments, suggestions and recommendations are welcomed: Ori@Ori-and-Ricki.net

What else can you do?

* The countdown to the actual moving day is a stressful time for everyone. During that period you may not have extra time for your child. To involve the child in the move, we suggest a type of Moving Advent Calendar. For the 30 days before the move, each day shows either a surprise, a reminder, or a task. You need one envelope per day marked with the date. Put the instructions or surprise in the envelopes. Attach the envelopes to a cord in a visible place. An example: one of the tasks can be to design and prepare the invitations for the goodbye party. This step-by-step approach prepares the child for what is coming and adds a feeling of suspension and surprise to what is otherwise an intangible move regarded with trepidation.

* Encourage your child to read famous children's books such as Nils Holgersson, the Wizard of Oz, Alice in Wonderland or Peter Pan. The figures in these books travel too and master new challenges. It is just a small step from fantasy to the reality of their life.

* The (best) friends of your children are also opinion makers. Ask them over to watch a video on the new country and have some travel brochures for them to look at. A positive reaction from the friends will resonate within your child.

* Invite a family (or a recently returned expatriate family) from your new destination country, preferably with children of the same age. Use this as a debriefing opportunity and let the children take an active part in this face-to-face session.

* Oh dear, the pet can't go. Ensure that your child is convinced that the solution found is the best one. Let him or her take pictures with the new owners / caretakers, and ask them to send an update on the well-being of the animal.

* Depending on your destination, certain preferred (food) products or (clothing) articles may not be available. Ask local expats or consult an expat organisation so that you can stock up on these items. (Please do check the local import regulations / duties). Contact for clubs: **www.fawco.org** Internet shopping at specialised retailers who carry typical preferred foods and will send by mail is now widely available, see: **www.expatshopping.com**

* Contact the new school / grade before the move. Have your child either mail or send a picture with a short description of his or her present routine and interests. In most of the cases the return answer is very positive and takes a lot of anxiety away.

Chapter 3 : Staying in touch and finding new friends

* Give "the staying in touch intention" a helping hand. Distribute self-addressed and pre-stamped postcards to the parents of your child's friends. This is a simple way of assisting the children to deliver on the promise they made.

* Another user-friendly method of staying in touch is to have a family homepage or newsletter. Have your family members submit copy, i.e. a drawing, a funny story, etc. for quarterly updates. This can easily be copied and sent to the large constituency back home, either by post, fax, E-mail or simply put on your family homepage.

* A "linked-friends" E-mail: like any circular letter, but strictly amongst friends, with a maximum of five in the circle; each friend

adds to it with his or her comments and views before sending it off to the next in line. Once the fifth person has added his or her remarks it is returned to the originator showing all the thoughts included as the communication circulated among the five friends.

* Whenever possible use the school holidays to either invite a friend/relative from the home country to come over or to have your child visit the home country for part of the school vacation.

Chapter and : Life in the new country

* Many international schools offer a summer programme for new arrivals – students get to know each other and, also, certain "lacking" subjects are covered. Please inquire during your look-and-see trip.

* Stimulate curiosity and learning by offering attendance at a foreign language summer camp facilitated by language schools. Another tangible way to introduce your new host culture is to try out a typical meal or snack once a week.

* Prepare your child for a range of other cultural experiences. Depending on your destination pay attention to:
  - the value system used towards (domestic) animals; which animals are considered as pets and which are consumed.
  - the impact of outer appearance; this includes (appropriate) clothing, jewellery and other body ornamentations.
  - the concept of (personal) hygiene, which can vary in methods used and definitions of cleanliness.
  - the level of respect and its implementation towards women, children, and elderly people and guests.
  - the economic spread in a society; the gap between rich and poor may vary from that in your home country.

- the expected accepted public behaviour; this includes not only verbal but also non-verbal communication, such as eye contact, touching and the display of emotions.
- the importance of religion and the presence of religious rites and rituals in everyday life.

* When confronted with the unknown, train the follow approach:
  1) Describe what you see without putting a value on the observed.
  2) Analyse the observed; what do I think it is, what does it mean?
  3) What do you feel or experience?
  This way rational questioning is brought forward and an emotional judgement is delayed. Avoid premature, possibly biased cultural judgements and encourage the development of intercultural under-standing.

* Practise the above by watching the Walt Disney video of "Pocah ontas", where intellectual curiosity, critical thinking, and tolerance is the central theme. The book "People" by Peter Spier is also a good resource to show the richness offered by diversity.

* Pay attention to clothing that is worn to school. Clarify the impor-tance of brand-name clothing and what is considered appropriate, so that you can get that important first impression right.

* Familiarise the children with everyday routines (traffic, telephone systems, the way home). Page 70 contains space for important information and contact addresses. This or a similar format is best carried by the child for the first six months. Also make sure your child knows how to handle the local money.

* If it applies, discuss within the family the effects caused by: daily routine changes caused by dual career challenges, extensive travel-ling by one of the spouses, the distance/time involved in getting to school, and living in company housing!

* Explain that "home-sickness" is normal. It affects both large and small. Your first priority is settling-in. Make sure it will start to feel like home by truly familiarising yourself with the direct neigh- bourhood. Wait with the big trips until you are acquainted with the local area.

* A phase of retreat is to be expected. In this book you will find activities that your child can enjoy on his or her own. On page 75 the child is reminded to unpack the remaining boxes. Pack a sur- prise kit of window color® painting supplies into the moving carton marked by your child as low priority. Page 80 holds an Ori pattern; with the surprise, this could be a jumpstart to get active again.

* Many children dread the first day at school; suggest the Global Three-in-a-Row form to the new teacher, see page 78. It offers a playful way of getting to know each other.

* Every child will react in his or her own individual way to an inter- national move. Should you observe out of the norm behaviour such as sleeping or eating disorders, aggressive behaviour at home or at school, overtly headstrong actions, crying, regression and / or clinging, these are typical symptoms of overload. Decrease the pace, do not push, allow enough time for rest and try to uphold certain routines for much needed orientation by the child.

* During this period of adjustment, plan if possible the visit of a friend from "home". Encourage your child to plan local outings, see page 79. By adopting the role of tour guide he or she will most likely realise that he or she has become a local expert in the eyes of the friend. The increased self-esteem generally leads to a higher identification with the host culture.

* To facilitate the reintegration into school, it is best to address the teacher before your departure. Depending on the destination and or choice of schools your child is likely to show deficits in national grammar, national history and national geography. There are special homeschooling options available.

* As the new "kid on the block", a presentation in front of his or her class about the experiences abroad saves the child from having to repeat his or her personal life story time and again.

* Careful! Refrain the child from constantly talking about his or her life abroad. This could easily be misunderstood as boasting or even hidden criticism for the home country culture. The presentation takes care of it in one go, and it is best when the child understands this.

* Ask the teacher for special support to help your child acclimatise – be it with extra homework for certain subjects and even more important, by not exposing the child should he or she have developed an accent, a different mode of speech, or a different view or way of doing things.

* Organise an exchange platform where other (repatriated) children share in each others' experiences.

* Check for a local chapter of the TCK network: Third Culture Kid: **www.tckworld.com** or alternatively Global Nomads under **www.tckinteract.net**

Ten-Point Action Plan

1. Involve the children at an early stage; the earlier the better, a time horizon of four months is ideal. Speak with the children about the host culture and what awaits the family in the new country. Give the children a chance to be in charge of parts of their preparations for moving rather than deciding on their behalf. Try to minimise fear of the unknown.

2. Both parents should display a positive yet realistic attitude, as this resonates within the family. With this in mind, be careful what you say; the smallest negative comment overheard bounces back at a later point in time.

3. The concerns of children when confronted with a move differ from those of parents. The child's initial focus is on the losing of friends followed by the major challenge of finding new ones. The concerns of the parents hover around the education and school performance of the children.
   Please do not underestimate the stress felt on the part of your child.

4. When possible, avoid implementing other changes during this time of flux, i.e. new school subjects, a family separation, etc. These multiple layers inhibit a rapid integration, whereas continuity will assist this process.

5. Consistency is also important on the home front. Your specific family rules and code of conduct should be maintained even when at times it seems that all other matters are at loose ends.

6. Encourage your children to keep their friendships.

7. Help and actively support your children in the finding of new friends.

8. Be aware that the time involved for adaptation after a move is three to four months. Add more time when your move has taken your family to a foreign language culture.

9. Be prepared for a performance loss at school during the first six months. Please show understanding by having patience and confidence in the future. Especially high achievement seekers need to be warned about a possible performance decline.

10. Most domestic accidents take place after the first six months. Have your security and safety precautions up and running all the time.

Source: Prof. Stefan Hormuth, Gutachten für das Auswärtige Amt, Gießen, 1988

Tap into these sources

Generic Information on raising a family abroad:

* Culture Shock! Successful Living Abroad: A Parent's Guide   ISBN 1-55868-425-5
* Moving Your Family Overseas, Rosalid Kalb & Penelope Welch   ISBN 1-877864-14-5
* Notes from a Traveling Childhood,
  the Foreign Service Youth Foundation   ISBN 0-9658538-1-0
* How Children Learn and Unlearn Prejudices, Anti-Defamation league   ISBN 0-439-21121-2
* The Third Culture Kid Experience, David Pollock & Ruth van Reken ISBN:1-877864-72-2
* **www.tckworld.com** and **www.transition-dynamics.com** reach out to the tck community.

Children's books:

* The Wizard of Oz, L. Frank Baum   ISBN 0-694-01319-6
* The Wonderful Adventures of Nils Holgerssons, Selma Lagerlöf   ISBN 0-486-28611-8
* Peter Pan, James M. Barrie   ISBN 0-140-36674-1
* Alice in Wonderland, Lewis Carroll   ISBN 0-192-83374-X
* Children Just Like Me, Celebrations! Barnabas & Anabel Kindersley ISBN 0-7894-2027-9
* Favorite Folktales from Around the World, Jane Yolen   ISBN 0-394-75188-4
* Passport on a Plate, a Round the World Cookbook, Diane Simone Vezza ISBN 0-689-80155-6
* How do you spell God? Marc Gellman   ISBN 0-606-13493-X
* People, Peter Spier   ISBN 0-385-24669-X
* Let's Move Together, Carol Schubeck   ISBN 0-9675567-0-8
* Pocahontas, an Indian Legend, Walt Disney's videos

Creativity books and sources:

* Yami's Origami, Yami Yamauchi   ISBN 1-89059700-7
* String Games from Around the World, Anne Akers Johnson   ISBN 1-57054040-3
* The Multicultural Game Book, Louise Orlando   ISBN 0-590-49409-0-7
* For window-color-painting visit **www.misterart.com**

Educational resources for children:

* www.theschoolreport.com
* www.rsts.net/home
* www.startribune.com/education/homework
* www.K12nation.net

Websites:

* www.travelwithyourkids.com
* www.Berlitz.com/kidtalk
* www.sausagetools.com/junior
* www.iecc.org
* www.kidsreport.com
* www.scout.net
* www.earthcalendar.net
* www.countryreports.org
* www.expatshopping.com
* www.hilink.com.au/times
* http://sunsite.berkeley.edu/kidsclick
* www.kidsdomain.com
* www.cybersleuth-kids.com
* www.thinkquest.org
* www.yahooligans.com
* www.holidayfestival.com
* www.fawco.org
* www.tckinteract.net

Prudent parent disclaimer

1. Content

Whilst we have taken reasonable care with the contents of the book, the information contained does not make any recommendation upon which you can rely without further personal consideration. The authors, editors and publisher reserve the right not to be responsible for the topicality, correctness, completeness or quality of the information provided. Liability claims regarding damage caused by the use of any information provided, including any kind of information which is incomplete or incorrect, will therefore be rejected, except in case of wrongful intent on the part of the authors, editors and or the publisher. Parts of the pages or the complete publication including all offers and information might be extended, changed or partly or completely deleted without separate announcement.

2. Referrals and links

The authors, editors and publisher are not responsible for any contents linked or referred to from this page. The above mentioned websites are not under their control and they are therefore not responsible for the contents or any links contained in these websites. If any damage occurs by the use of information presented there, only the author of the respective pages might be liable, not the one who has linked to these websites. We provide these addresses as a convenience only. You assume total responsibility in terms of privacy, personal safety, damage, loss and or liability when visiting the websites and or during the enacting of the activities in the book. Furthermore the publisher is not liable for any postings or messages published by users of discussion boards, guestbooks or mailinglists provided on this page.
Be a smart parent and look over the shoulder of your children and use your sound judgement.

My personal action plan

My personal action plan

My personal action plan

My personal action plan

My personal action plan

My personal action plan

My personal action plan